Highlights

On-the-Go Jokes

Why Did the Chicken Cross the Road?

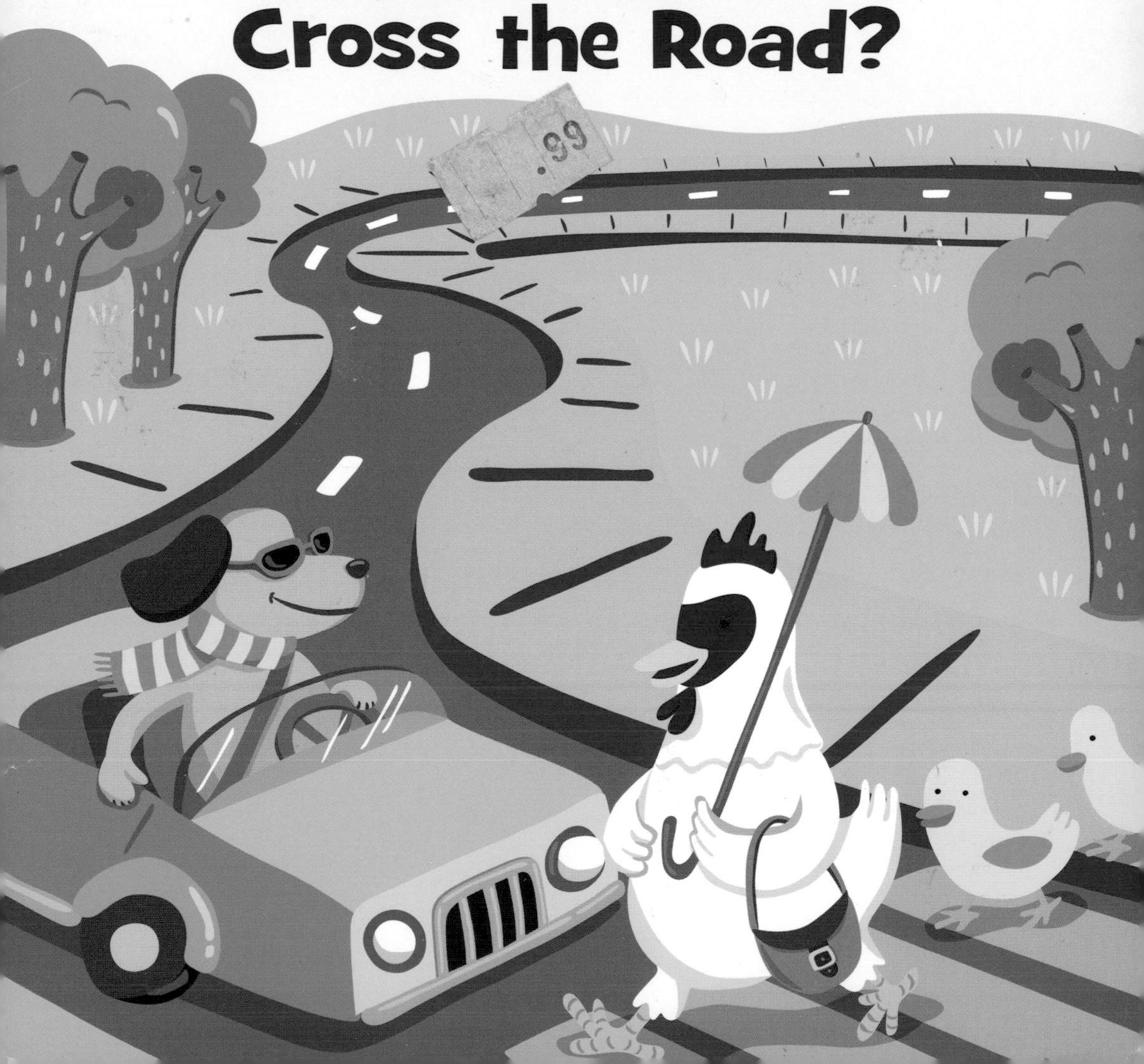

In this joke and puzzle pad filled with things on the move, you'll decode riddles, solve ciphers, test out tricky tongue twisters, and puzzle your way to a laugh attack. You'll also find Hidden Pictures®, wacky word puzzles, silly picture puzzles, and other zany activities.

What runs through a city without moving? Drive on over to page 11 to find out.

Why do birds fly south for the winter? Solve the Hidden Pictures® puzzle code on page 36 for the answer.

What do you call a story about boats? Decipher the flag code on page 43 for the punch line.

The *Purr*-fect Trip

These cats are hightailing it out of town and on to their vacation spot. To find out where they're headed, read the road signs. The direction of the arrow on each sign tells you to count the letters to the right or left. The mile number tells you how many letters to count. The first word is done to start you on the right road.

T H E   ___ ___ ___ ___ ___ ___

___ ___ ___ ___ ___ ___ ___

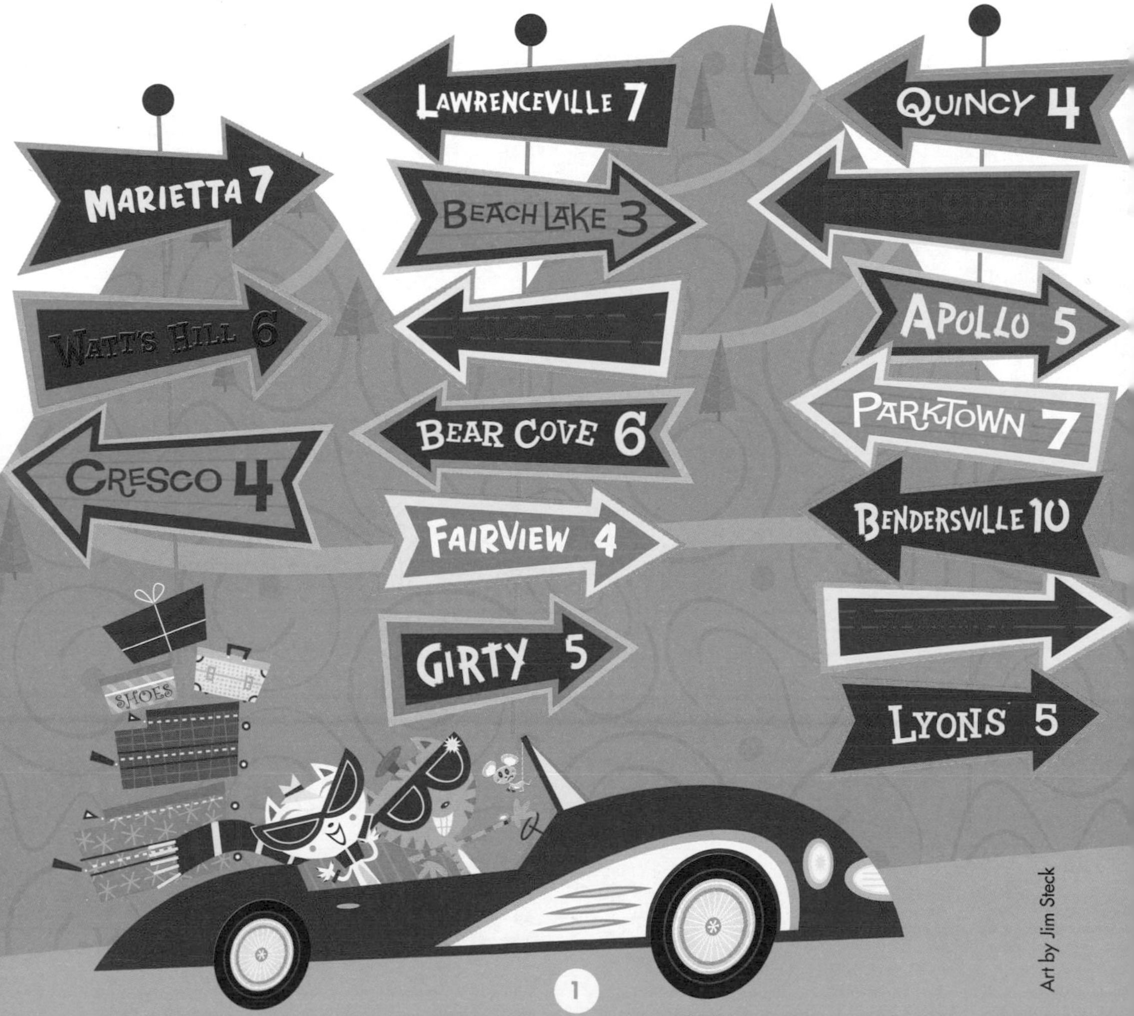

Art by Jim Steck

In-Flight Snickers

Where are the Great Plains?
At the great airports

How do rabbits travel?
By hareplane

Why do pilots always fly past Peter Pan's island?
Because the sign says "Neverland"

How many pairs of shoes does a jet plane need?
Enough for 30,000 feet

What did the pilot eat for a snack?
Plane yogurt

Where do chickens like to sit on a plane?
The wing

PASSENGER ON PLANE: Those people down there look like ants!
FLIGHT ATTENDANT: They are ants. We haven't left the ground yet.

Art by Pete Whitehead

Where R U Going?

Planes are about to take off from this airport—but where are they going? Sound out each U.S. city name on the sign. Then find the passenger who's going there by unscrambling the state names on the suitcases.

Art by Dave Whamond

What's Wrong?®

Which things in this picture are silly? It's up to you!

Art by Gary LaCoste

Critter Cruise

As this ship stops at each port, passengers get on and off. For example, at the first port in Kitty City, four board and no one leaves. How many passengers will be aboard after Birdboro?

PORT	BOARD	LEAVE
Kitty City	4	0
Dogdale	2	1
Bunniopolis	0	3
Hamstershire	6	1
Ponyport	2	0
Birdboro	0	1

TED: How did you like the cruise?
NED: It was fun, but I didn't like the washing machines on the walls.
TED: They weren't washing machines; they were portholes!
NED: No wonder I didn't get my clothes back.

Puzzle by Kevin McPartland
Art by Pat Lewis

Hidden Pictures®

Find these objects hidden in the big picture. Then use the object code and letters to solve the riddle.

A	B	C	E	H
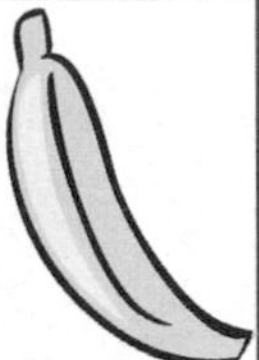 banana	 bow	 rake	 bell	 apple core

L	O	S	T	V
 envelope	 kite	 fork	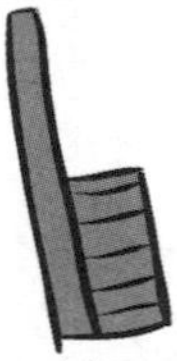 toothbrush	 worm

What do maps and fish have in common?

_ _ _ _   _ _ _ _   _ _ _ _ _ _ _ _.

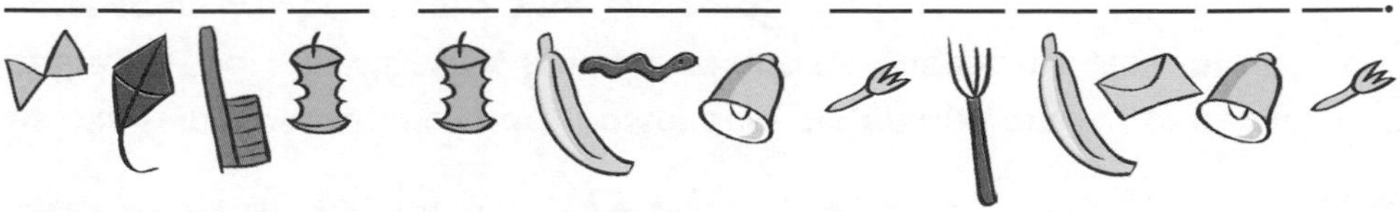

Art by Jackie Stafford

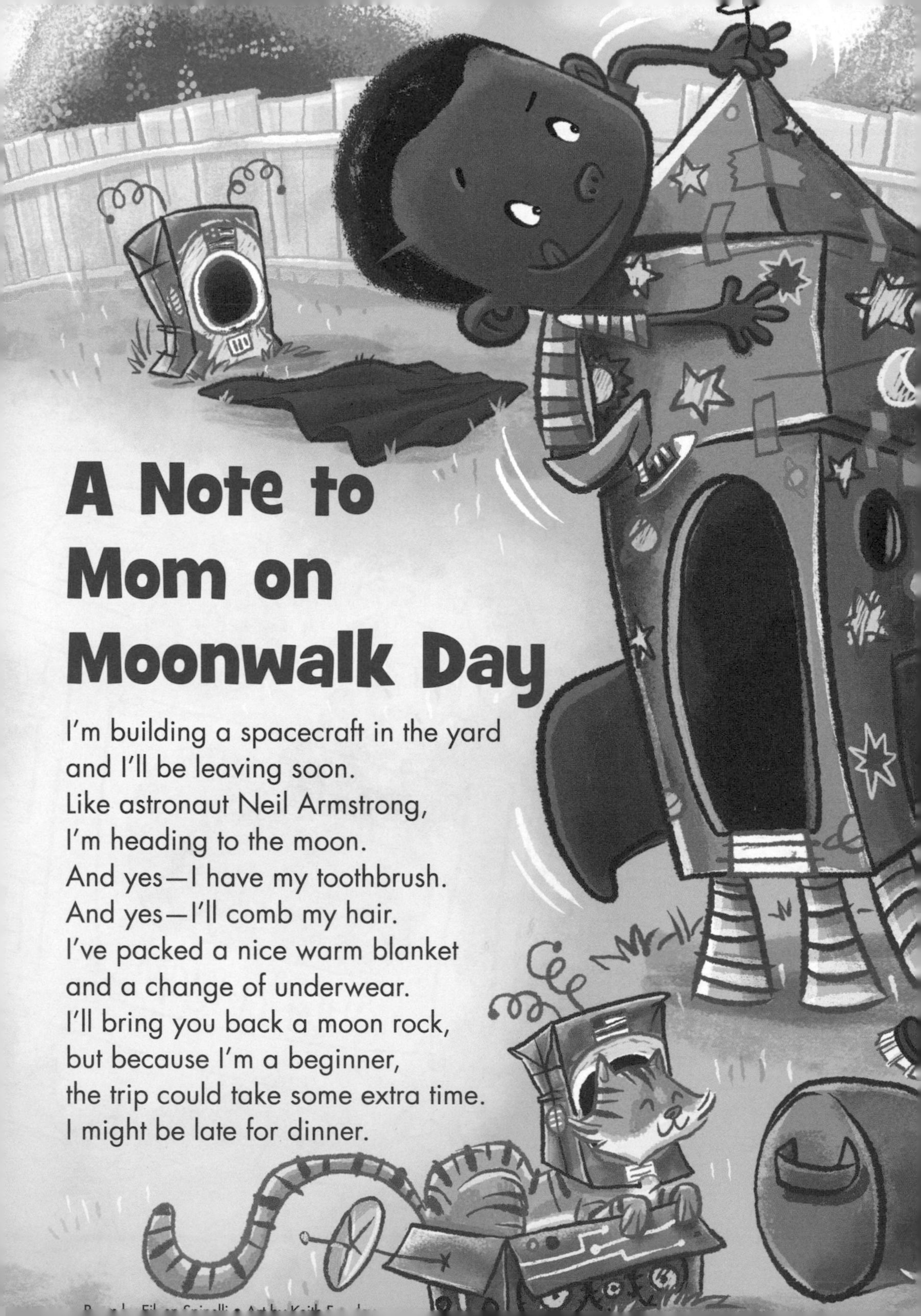

A Note to Mom on Moonwalk Day

I'm building a spacecraft in the yard
and I'll be leaving soon.
Like astronaut Neil Armstrong,
I'm heading to the moon.
And yes—I have my toothbrush.
And yes—I'll comb my hair.
I've packed a nice warm blanket
and a change of underwear.
I'll bring you back a moon rock,
but because I'm a beginner,
the trip could take some extra time.
I might be late for dinner.

Reading Space

Do you know what astronauts like to read? Follow each line from a letter to a blank space and write the letter in that space. When you are finished, you will have the answer to the riddle.

Art by Mike Moran

At the Bus Stop

What did the bus driver say to the frog?
"Hop on!"

Knock, knock.
Who's there?
Stacey.
Stacey who?
Stacey'ted until the bus stops.

What do you get when you cross a watermelon with a bus?
A fruit that can seat forty-five people

CUSTOMER: I'd like to buy a trap, and please hurry, because I need to catch the bus.
CLERK: I'm sorry, sir, but we don't carry traps that large.

What is a bus you can never enter?
A syllabus

Knock, knock.
Who's there?
Wafer.
Wafer who?
Wafer the bus at the corner.

What lives in the sea and
carries a lot of people?
An octobus

Art by Arthur Lin

City Sounds

Can you solve this code using the sounds of the city? Figure out the clues to find out the answer to the riddle.

1. This vowel appears twice on the rails.
2. You'll find this letter at the end of a nutty noise.
3. This vowel is the second letter in a car sound.
4. This letter is the first out of the dog's mouth.
5. This letter appears three times in a musical sound.

What runs through a city without moving?

___ ___ ___ ___ ___
4 3 1 5 2

Art by Tim Bradford

Vacation Destinations

Each suitcase has one that matches it exactly. Pair up the suitcases to match each traveler with its destination.

____ **1.** Where does bacteria go on vacation?

____ **2.** Where do termites go on vacation?

____ **3.** Where do cows go on vacation?

____ **4.** Where do sneakers go on vacation?

____ **5.** Where do ants go on vacation?

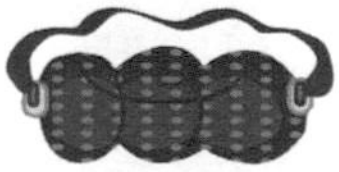

____ **6.** Where do cars go on vacation?

____ **7.** Where do ghosts go on vacation?

____ **8.** Where do pencils go on vacation?

A. Lace Vegas

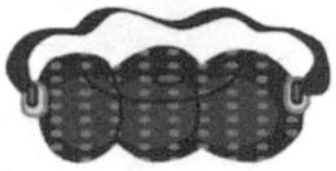

B. Key West

C. Pennsylvania

D. Hollywood

E. The Boohamas

F. Moo York

G. Germany

H. Frants

Art by Mike Dammer

Family Vacations

Three families went on vacation. The Kings, the Greens, and the Peñas each have two children, and each family went to a different place. Use the clues to figure out where each family went and what the children's last names are.

Use the chart to keep track of your answers.
For example, the first clue says that William's last name is Green.
Write "Green" in the last name box for William.

	Jennifer	Daniel	Mia	William	Mike	Emily
Last Name						
New York City						
Hawaii						
Alaska						

1. William's last name is Green.
2. The Peña children's names begin with **M**.
3. Emily and Daniel went to the same place.
4. The King children brought back shells for souvenirs.
5. Jennifer bought a model of the Statue of Liberty.

Art by David Coulson

How do you find out the weather when you're on vacation?
Look out the window.

All Aboard!

Hop on the joke train! To solve each riddle, start at the arrow. Write every other letter in order in the spaces below, crossing out each letter once it's been used. Keep going until you've been to each letter exactly once. Hurry up before the train leaves the station!

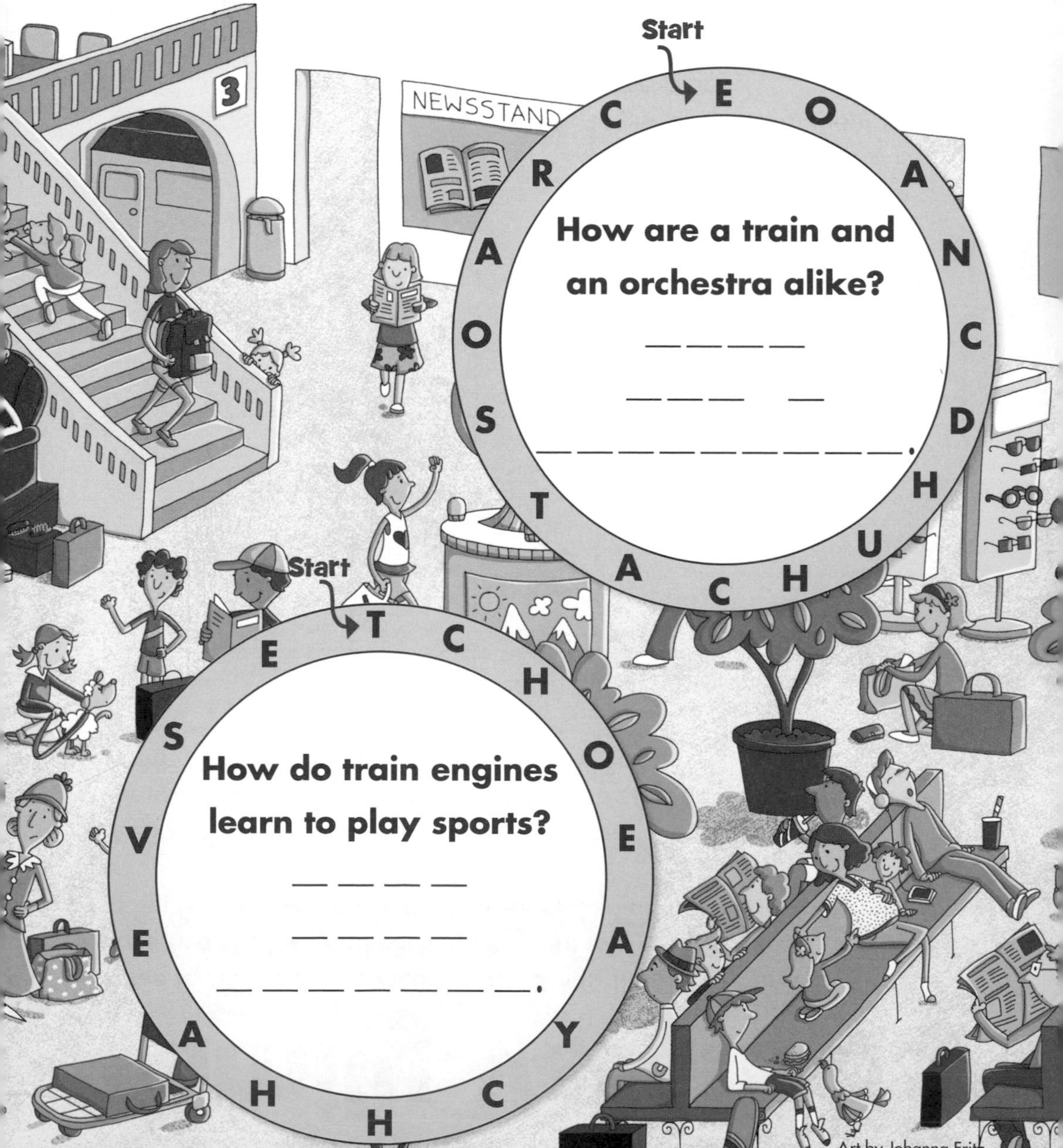

Art by Johanna Fritz

Riddle Sudoku

Fill in the squares so that the six letters appear only once in each row, column, and 2 x 3 box. Then read the blue squares to find out the answer to the riddle.

Our Sudoku puzzles use letters instead of numbers.

Riddle: What does a choo-choo train need?

Letters: A H E K N I

	E		N	A	
N			I		
K			E		
		A			
A		E			N
I	N	H		K	

Answer: A ___ ___ ___ ___ ___ ___

Art by Patrick Girouard

Good Advice

If stuck behind an elephant,
Don't stomp your feet.
Don't rave and rant.
Just look around, enjoy the view!
There's really nothing else to do.
You'll soon discover that you can't
Hurry up an elephant.

Poem by Marileta Robinson • Art by BB Sams

Elephant Crossing

To cross the road and get the answer to the riddle below, first cross out all the pairs of matching letters. Then write the remaining letters in order in the spaces next to the riddle.

QQ	BE	EE	NN	MM	OO	WW
LL	CA	SS	VV	YY	US	ZZ
ET	AA	RR	NN	HE	EE	YY
HH	XX	YL	DD	PP	UU	OV
GG	OO	ET	SS	CC	QQ	II
CC	RA	EE	MM	AA	TT	VE
LI	BB	KK	VV	ZZ	NG	TT

Why do elephants have trunks?

Art by Brian White

Tongue Tied!

Put your helmet on and take these tongue twisters for a ride. Can you say each five times fast?

Blake's bike is bigger, but Betty's bike is better.

Whoosh whirred the wheels on Wren's ride.

Brooke bought a bright blue bike.

Greg's green helmet helps him.

Riley rides the roads after Rose rides.

Doug double-dog dares Dawn downhill.

Poppy passes pretty ponies on the path.

Even when one of Juan's wheels was wobbly, he still won!

Art by Kevin Zimmer

Trail Treading

Can you help Evelyn get to the end of the mountain-bike trail?

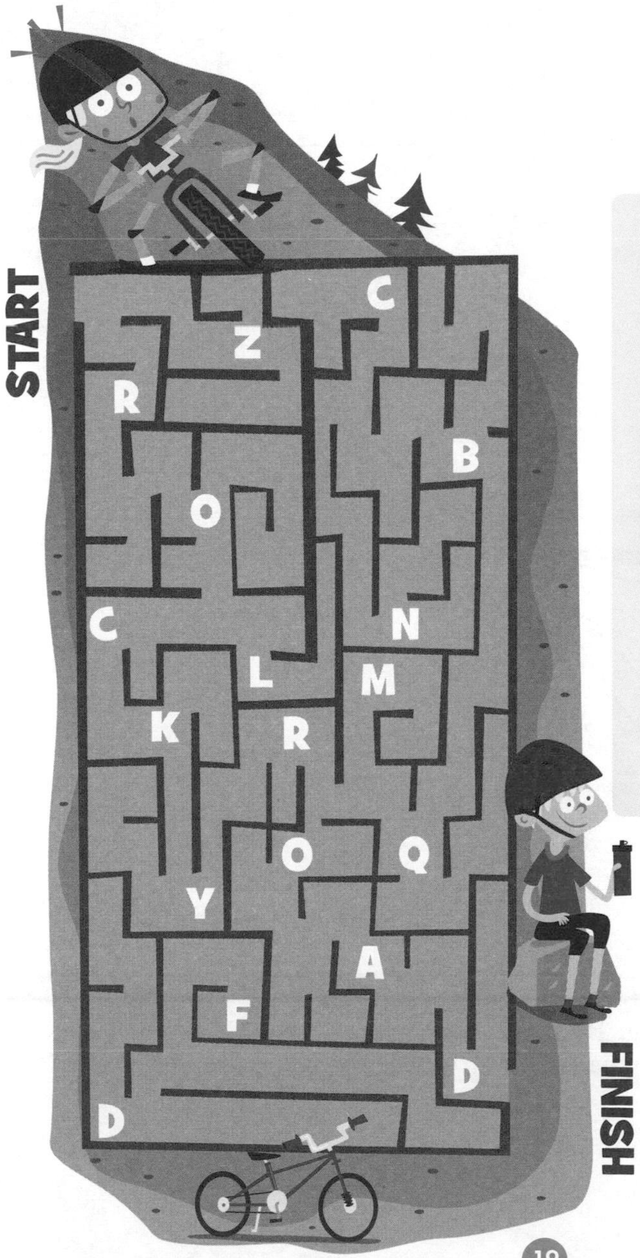

Once you've found the correct path, write the letters along it in order in the spaces below. They'll answer this riddle.

What ice-cream flavor do bikers like the least?

___ ___ ___ ___ ___

___ ___ ___ ___

Art by Mike Moran

Just Sayin' . . .

Give this bird something to say. Then search the Hidden Pictures® puzzle for the hidden CHAIR, FISH, MARKER, SLICE OF PIZZA, and STOPWATCH.

Art by James Kochalka

The "You Night Did" States

Ethan and his pen pal, Melanie, like to make up codes. In his recent letter, Ethan made up codes for 10 state names. Can you crack them?
Hint: Sound them out!

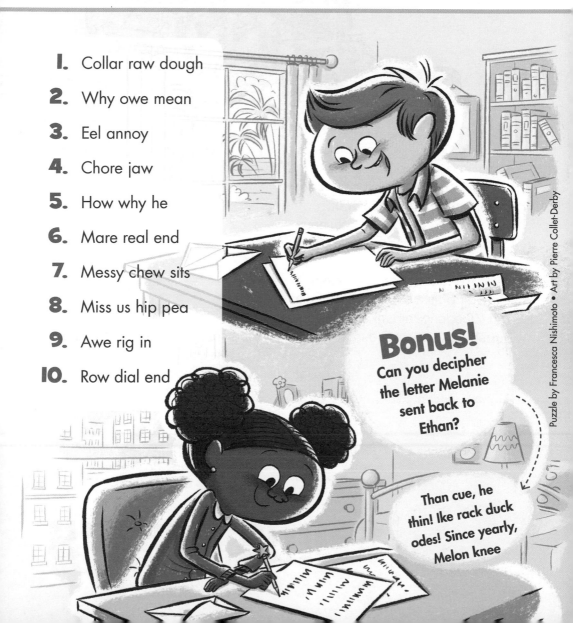

1. Collar raw dough
2. Why owe mean
3. Eel annoy
4. Chore jaw
5. How why he
6. Mare real end
7. Messy chew sits
8. Miss us hip pea
9. Awe rig in
10. Row dial end

Puzzle by Francesca Nishimoto • Art by Pierre Collet-Derby

Safari Sillies

Imagine you're on safari and a lion is chasing you. What do you do?
Stop pretending!

ELEPHANT 1: Did you hear about the race between the two giraffes?
ELEPHANT 2: I heard it was neck and neck!

Knock, knock.
Who's there?
Safari.
Safari who?
Safari so good!

What do you call a truck full of bison?
A buffa-load

Knock, knock.
Who's there?
Rhino.
Rhino who?
Rhino every knock-knock joke there is.

A lost explorer was wandering through the jungle. Suddenly, he came face to face with a lion. The explorer was so scared that he fainted.

When he woke, the lion was kneeling beside him.

"Thank you for not eating me," the man said to the lion.

"Hush," the lion replied, "I'm saying grace."

Art by Kevin Rechin

Boating Blunders

What did the boy get when he leaned over the back of the boat? To find out, follow the directions below. Each sentence will tell you where one letter is in the grid. Once you've found it, write it in the correct space below the riddle.

1. This letter is three down from the **X**.
2. This letter is the only vowel in the second row.
3. This letter is two up from the **Q**.
4. This letter is sandwiched between two **E**'s.
5. This is the second letter in the last row.
6. This letter is the first and last in its row.
7. This letter appears side by side in the same row.
8. This letter is the first letter in the grid.
9. This letter is the only consonant in its column.

R	P	A	X	A	L	Z
T	A	B	F	W	G	M
S	Z	J	F	E	W	S
K	H	O	T	O	I	D
B	N	M	R	I	G	G
Y	E	N	E	U	Q	C

What did the boy get when he leaned over the back of the boat?

__   __ __ __ __ __   __ __ __ __ __ __ __

2   6 1 5 8 4   9 2 8 4 3 4 7

Art by Scott Angle

What's Wrong?®

Which things in this picture are silly? It's up to you!

Art by Mitch Mortimer

Check . . . and Double Check

There are at least 16 differences in these pictures. How many can you find?

Art by Kelly Kennedy

Out-of-This-World Humor

These comet-dians are passing time in space by telling jokes.

Art by Garry Colby

Road Trip on Planet Paint

On Planet Paint, color rules! To travel around, you must leave any purple house by a road that's a different color from the one you came in on. How many moves will it take you to get from START to FINISH?

START
FINISH
BONUS:
Are there more green, orange, or pink paintbrushes hidden in this picture?

Puzzle by James Vorosmarti • Art by Joey Ellis

Hidden Pictures®

Find these objects hidden in the big picture. Then use the object code and letters to solve the riddle.

A	D	E	F	I
kite	flying disc	horseshoe	banana	saltshaker

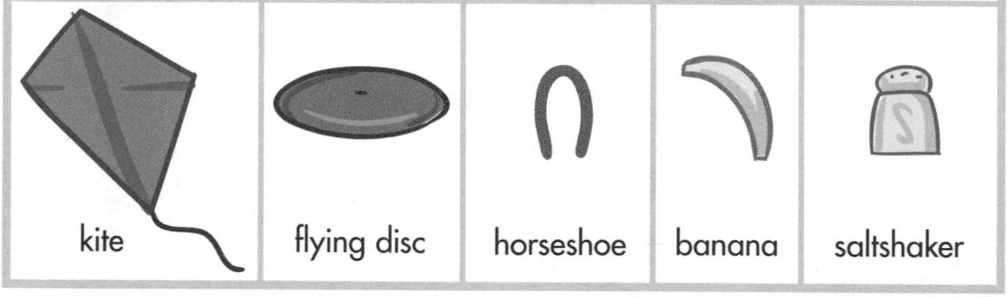

L	P	R	S	T
teddy bear	spatula	fish	egg	needle

KNOCK, KNOCK.
WHO'S THERE?

___ ___ ___ ___ ___ ___ ___.

___ ___ ___ ___ ___ ___ ___ ***WHO?***

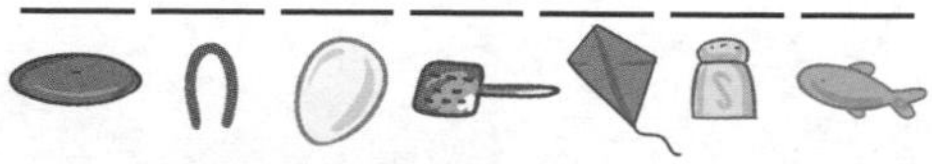

___ ___ ___ ___ ___ ___ ___ ___ ___ ___ ___ ___ ___

___ ___ ___ ___!

Art by Dave Clegg

World Pieces

What travels around the world but never leaves its corner? To find out, rearrange the letters in each of the phrases below to spell the name of a country. Then write the numbered letters in the answer spaces at the bottom of the page.

1. MICE OX (North America) ___ ___ ___ ___ ___ ___
(1 under the 1st blank)

2. NEAR GIANT (South America)

___ ___ ___ ___ ___ ___ ___ ___ ___
(3 under the 6th blank)

3. WE SEND (Europe) ___ ___ ___ ___ ___ ___
(2 under the 1st blank)

4. HI OAT PIE (Africa) ___ ___ ___ ___ ___ ___ ___ ___
(5 under the 6th blank)

5. A HAND LIT (Asia) ___ ___ ___ ___ ___ ___ ___ ___
(4 under the 3rd blank)

What travels around the world but never leaves its corner?

___   ___ ___ ___ ___ ___
4   2 3 4 1 5

Art by Kelly Kennedy

Robot Vacation

Cross out all the boxes in which the number can be evenly divided by **3**. Then write the leftover letters in the spaces to spell the answer.

33 H	31 T	9 R	17 O	13 R	42 Q	8 E	27 Z	10 C	39 A	91 H
24 B	54 Y	37 A	55 R	12 L	2 G	60 W	11 E	18 M	23 H	77 I
30 F	43 S	36 N	22 B	35 A	90 E	3 O	38 T	21 K	5 T	99 S
81 D	18 V	43 E	45 C	53 R	15 J	28 I	46 E	54 P	6 B	19 S

Why did the robot go on vacation?

___ ___   ___ ___ ___ ___ ___ ___ ___ ___

___ ___ ___   ___ ___ ___ ___ ___ ___ ___ ___ ___

Art by Chuck Dillon

Traffic Laughs

What kind of food has cars and trucks in it?
Traffic jam

Knock, knock.
Who's there?
Cargo.
Cargo who?
Cargo "beep beep!"

What did the traffic light say to the car?
"Don't look! I'm changing."

Knock, knock.
Who's there?
Tire.
Tire who?
Tire shoe before you trip!

Why are police officers the strongest people in the world?
Because they can hold up traffic with one hand

A book never written: *Are We There Yet?* by Mindy Carr.

Art by Nathan Jarvis

Rush Hour

It's rush hour—but take all the time you need to find:

- **two matching dresses, plants, and lizards**
- **a toad being towed**
- **a moose eating mousse**
- **a sail for sale**

Bonus!

Find these hidden objects: pink purse, red magnet, white candle, light gray cane and flowerpot, and dark gray shoe.

Art by Mary Sullivan

Just Sayin' . . .

Give this superhero something to say. Then search the Hidden Pictures® puzzle for the hidden APPLE, DOMINO, DOUGHNUT, FOOTBALL, RULER, and OPEN BOOK.

Art by Felipe Galindo Gomez

Letter Road

Drive around these roads to find the three letters that have an exact duplicate. Once you find all three letters, unscramble them to solve this riddle.

What has cities without houses, rivers without water, and forests without trees?

A ___ ___ ___

Hidden Pi

Find these objects hidden in the big picture. Then use
letters to solve the riddle.

A	F	I	K	
kite	broom	spoon	envelope	snake

O	R	S	T	W
ice-cream cone	piece of popcorn	computer mouse	glove	artist's brush

Why do birds fly south for the winter?

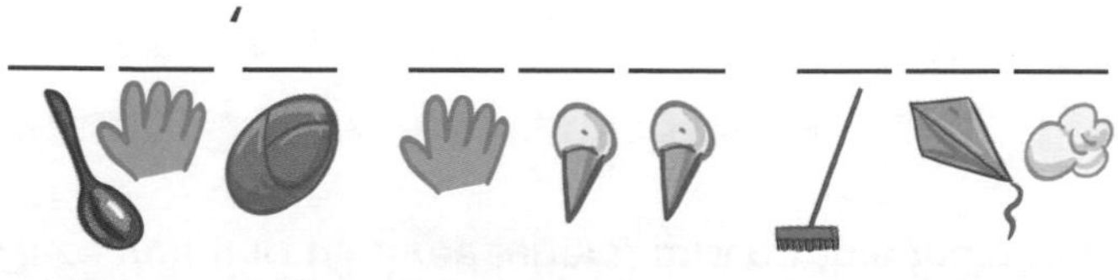

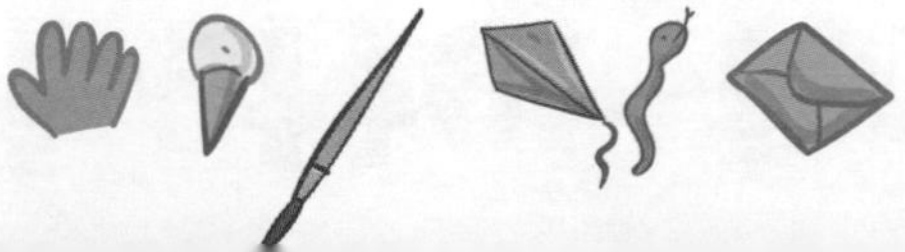

Art by Dave Clegg

Compass Code

How good is your sense of direction? To answer the riddle below, start at the North (**N**) circle. Then move in the directions listed and write the letters you find in the correct spaces. Get cracking before the sun goes down!

Where's the best place to eat while hiking?

Where there's

1. S 1 __A__

2. SE 2 ______
3. W 3 ______
4. NW 1 ______
5. S 3 ______

6. NE 3 ______
7. W 1 ______

8. S 2 ______
9. N 1 ______
10. SE 2 ______

11. W 3 ______
12. N 1 ______
13. E 2 ______
14. NW 2 ______

Art by Gary LaCoste

Getting Around

Circle the 18 types of transportation from the word list. They are hidden up, down, across, and diagonally. Then write the leftover letters in order from left to right and top to bottom. They will spell out the answer to the riddle.

Word List

BIKE
CANOE
CAR
KAYAK
MOTORCYCLE
PLANE
ROWBOAT
SAILBOAT
SCOOTER
SHIP
SUBWAY
TAXI
TRACTOR
TRAIN
TRUCK
TUGBOAT
VAN
WAGON

T	U	G	B	O	A	T	R	H	M
E	A	R	B	K	U	R	E	O	S
S	A	O	C	I	O	S	T	N	H
C	U	U	B	T	K	O	O	I	I
I	R	B	C	W	R	E	O	A	P
T	X	A	W	C	O	E	C	R	S
H	R	A	Y	A	K	R	S	T	C
T	I	C	T	A	Y	V	A	N	A
S	L	R	Y	E	N	A	L	P	N
E	T	A	O	B	L	I	A	S	O
O	K	W	A	G	O	N	A	R	E

How does a lion paddle his canoe?

__ __   __ __ __ __   __ __ __   __ __ __ __.

Art by Jack Desrocher

Travel Travails

TYLER: I just flew in from Philadelphia.
DYLAN: Wow! Your arms must be tired.

A woman telephoned an airline office and asked, "How long does it take to get to Boston?"
The clerk said, "Just a minute."
"Thanks," said the woman as she hung up.

TRAVELER: I'd like a room and a bath.
CLERK: I can give you a room, but you'll have to take your own bath.

A man ran frantically down the ferry landing, leaped across six feet of water, and landed with a crash on the deck of the ferry.
"Phew," he gasped as he picked himself up, "I made it!"
"What's the hurry?" asked the deckhand. "This boat is coming in!"

PASSENGER: This ship is sinking.
CAPTAIN: That's correct, Madam. But don't worry. We're only a mile from land.
PASSENGER: A mile! In what direction?
CAPTAIN: Down.

A man walks into a railroad station and asks the ticket agent, "May I have a round-trip ticket, please?"
The ticket agent asks, "Where to?"
The man answers, "Back here again, of course!"

Art by Jack Desrocher

A Message from the Past

Crossing the country in a covered wagon is no laughing matter, but that doesn't mean the pioneers didn't have a sense of humor. Decipher the coded riddle below by putting the last letter of each word first and the first letter last.

yhW did eht sioneerp srosc eht yountrc ni doverec sagonw?

ecausB yhet did ton tanw ot taiw yortf seary rof a nrait

Art by Dave Klug

Popcorn Dream

Last night I had the strangest dream.
While boating on a lake,
I felt the ship begin to crunch,
the deck begin to shake!

The water that I sailed upon
had disappeared somehow.
And in its place, to my surprise,
as I looked past the bow,

the lake was filled with yellow puffs
on which my ship was borne.
I scarcely could believe my eyes!
Who popped this magic corn?

I thought of just one thing to do.
"Abandon ship!" I cried.
And as I headed overboard,
I opened my mouth wide.

Poem by Robert Schechter • Art by Rob McClurkan

Ferry Ride

What do you call a story about boats? Use this flag code to find the answer.

Art by Monica Wellington

Books Never Written

Check out the titles of these 10 funny books. See how many you can match with the author. (HINT: Try reading the authors' names out loud!)

____	1. *Moving Cars*	A. Austin N. Dallas
____	2. *Touring Arizona*	B. Carrie Maya Bags
____	3. *Journey Across the Sahara*	C. Wanda Rhode
____	4. *Safe Road Crossing*	D. Gran Canyon
____	5. *Not There Yet*	E. Rhoda Camel
____	6. *Exploring the Country*	F. Ike N. Fly
____	7. *A Tale of Two Texas Cities*	G. Minnie Sota
____	8. *A Heavy Load*	H. Otto Mo Biel
____	9. *The Land of 10,000 Lakes*	I. Luke Left and Den Wright
____	10. *How to Be a Pilot*	J. Myles A. Way

Art by Pete Whitehead

Truck Tunes

Use the number pairs to solve the riddle on this page. Move to the right to the first number and then up to the second number. Write the letters you find in the correct spaces.

Art by Garry Colby

What do long-distance truckers listen to?

◯◯◯◯◯ - ◯◯◯◯◯◯◯ ◯◯◯◯◯

1,7 4,2 2,5 8,6 5,4 9,9 7,3 4,8 6,6 2,3 4,2 7,8 3,6 9,2 8,6 3,9 1,7

Just Sayin' . . .

Give this student something to say. Then search the Hidden Pictures® puzzle for the hidden BANANA, ELEPHANT, MP3 PLAYER, PENCIL, and TOASTER.

Art by David Coulson

Riddle Sudoku

Fill in the squares so that the six letters appear only once in each row, column, and 2 x 3 box. Then read the green squares to find out the answer to the riddle.

Our Sudoku puzzles use letters instead of numbers.

Riddle: What only starts to work after it's fired?

Letters: O T E R C K

	K		E		
C					
	R		T	O	
	E	O		R	
					R
		R		K	

Answer: A __ __ __ __ __ __

Art by Jason Tharp

Car Carriers

Care to come along for a fun puzzle ride? Use the clues below to fill in the answer spaces. Each answer starts with the letters C-A-R. Now, carry on! Then put the numbered letters in the correct space below to solve the riddle.

1. Milk container — CAR__ __ __ (3rd blank: 2)
2. Orange veggie — CAR__ __ __ (3rd blank: 1)
3. Comic strip — CAR__ __ __ __
4. Feeling ill while driving — CAR__ __ __ __ (4th blank: 5)
5. Red bird — CAR__ __ __ __ __ (2nd blank: 3)
6. A fair — CAR__ __ __ __ __ (4th blank: 7)
7. Merry-go-round — CAR__ __ __ __ __ (1st blank: 4)
8. Meat eater — CAR__ __ __ __ __ __
9. A woodworker — CAR__ __ __ __ __ __ (1st blank: 6)

What would happen if all the cars in the country were painted pink?

It would be a __ __ __ __ CAR-__ __ __ __ __ __ .

6 3 2 5 — 2 7 1 3 4 2

Art by Kelly Kennedy

Freeway Free-for-All

Can you help Carl navigate the freeway to get home in time for dinner?

Once you've found the correct path, write the letters along it in order in the spaces below. They'll answer this riddle.

What driver never drives a car?

__   __ __ __ __ __ __ __ __ __ __ __ __

Art by Mike Moran

What's Wrong?®

Which things in this picture are silly? It's up to you!

Art by Mitch Mortimer

Hidden Words

There are six words (not pictures!) hidden in the scene below. Can you find them all? Once you do, arrange the words in order to give this knock-knock joke a punch line!

KNOCK, KNOCK.
WHO'S THERE?
CANOE.
CANOE WHO?

___ ___ ___ ___ ___   ___ ___ ___ ___

___ ___ ___   ___ ___ ___ ___   ___ ___ ___ ___ ___?

Art by Kelly Kennedy

Racecar Riddles

The race was won by a fraction of a second! Can you figure out the answers to these riddles? Each fraction tells you which letters to use.

1. What will the school for racecars do after the summer?

First $\frac{1}{2}$ of **READ**
Last $\frac{3}{5}$ of **KAZOO**
First $\frac{1}{4}$ of **MAIL**

__ __ - __ __ __ __

2. What did the hot dog say when it finished the race first?

Last $\frac{1}{2}$ of **TRIM**
First $\frac{3}{5}$ of **THEIR**
First $\frac{1}{2}$ of **WIND**
Last $\frac{2}{3}$ of **PEN**
Last $\frac{1}{3}$ of **MARKER**

"__'__ __ __ __ __ __ __ __ __ __!"

3. Where do racecars go to wash their clothes?

Last $\frac{3}{5}$ of **BATHE**
First $\frac{1}{2}$ of **LAMP**
Last $\frac{3}{4}$ of **FUND**
Last $\frac{1}{2}$ of **VERY**
First $\frac{1}{3}$ of **VET**
First $\frac{1}{2}$ of **ROSE**
Last $\frac{3}{5}$ of **BLOOM**

__ __ __ __ __ __ __ __ __ __ __ __ __ __ __ __ __

Art by Erin Mauterer

Truck Talk Box Drop

This grid contains a joke about a truck and its punch line. To read the joke, move the letters from each column into the boxes directly above them, staying in the same column. But watch out: the letters do not always go in the boxes in the same order as they appear. Each letter is used only once. We've filled in some to get you started. Put your seat belt on and fill in the rest!

W	H	A	T		D	I	D				
	T						A				
				D			V			?	
	“	G									
			B					.	”		

							~~V~~				
		~~A~~	~~B~~	~~D~~	E	S	M				
	~~H~~	I	R	E	A	K	~~D~~	E		A	
T	H	E	~~T~~	R	~~D~~	~~I~~	E	Y	R	T	E
~~W~~	~~T~~	~~G~~	I	V	R	I	~~A~~	E	T	H	O

Art by Garry Colby

My Vacation on Earth

This alien's postcard got scrambled in space. Can you unscramble each set of letters to decipher the message? Then use the code below to solve the riddle.

Dear Zatz,

We're having a great time on planet **TAHER**! But you won't believe how different things are here.

The **ZAZIP** is shaped like a **CRILEC**. Earthlings eat **NOREPIPEP** and **SHMOORUMS** as toppings.

The **MIMSWING** pools are filled with **RAWET**, and kids dive down instead of up.

I can't wait to show you all of the cool Earth **SKORC** I picked up when I get back **MEHO**! You'll never guess what color they are—gray!

Your friend,
Zurkle

Art by Pete Whitehead

TAHER ___ ___ ___ ___ ___
(2 under the 4th blank)

ZAZIP ___ ___ ___ ___ ___
(3 under the 1st blank)

CRILEC ___ ___ ___ ___ ___ ___
(6 under the 2nd blank)

NOREPIPEP ___ ___ ___ ___ ___ ___ ___ ___ ___
(10 under the 2nd blank; 7 under the 8th blank)

SHMOORUMS ___ ___ ___ ___ ___ ___ ___ ___ ___
(9 under the 1st blank; 4 under the 5th blank)

MIMSWING ___ ___ ___ ___ ___ ___ ___ ___
(8 under the 8th blank)

RAWET ___ ___ ___ ___ ___
(1 under the 2nd blank)

SKORC ___ ___ ___ ___ ___
(5 under the 4th blank)

MEHO ___ ___ ___ ___
(11 under the 2nd blank)

Where does an alien park his vehicle?

___ ___   ___   ___ ___ ___ ___ ___ ___ ___
1 2   1   3 1 4 5 6 7 8

___ ___ ___ ___ ___ ___
9 10 2 10 11 4

Traffic Laughs

A bus driver was driving the wrong way down a one-way street. Officer Wheeler stopped the bus and said to the driver, "Don't you see that one-way sign?"

The bus driver replied, "But, Officer, I *am* going only one way!"

Three guys were driving to the park. As they got closer, they saw a sign that said, "Park Left."

"Too bad," they said, and turned around to go back home.

A man was speeding, and a police officer pulled him over.

"I'm giving you a ticket for driving eighty-five miles per hour," the police officer said.

"What?" said the man. "I've only been driving for fifteen minutes."

"This is a dog license.
I need your driver's license."

Art by Norman Jung

Who's There?

Knock, knock! A traveling animal is at the door. It's up to you to crack the code and figure out this knock-knock joke. Each number stands for a different letter. Once you know one number's letter, you can fill in that letter each time you see that number. See who's at the door!

K N O C K, K N O C K.
1 2 3 4 1, 1 2 3 4 1

__ __ __' __   __ __ __ __ __?
5 6 3 ' 7   8 6 9 10 9

__ __ __ __ __ __.
11 12 13 11 4 11

__ __ __ __ __ __   __ __ __?
11 12 13 11 4 11   5 6 3

__ __ __ __ __ __   __ __ __   __ __ __ __ __,
11 12 13 11 4 11   8 6 9   8 10 14 2 1

__ __ __   __ __ __ __ – __   __ __ __
15 3 14   13 11 4 1 – 11   8 6 9

__ __ __ __ __ __ __ __.
7 14 16 8 4 11 7 9

Art by Mar Ferrero

Look Both Ways!

The chicken has all sorts of egg-cellent reasons for crossing the road: to prove she wasn't a chicken, to get to the other side, and many more. But why did other animals and objects cross the road? To find out, match up these riddles with their punch lines.

____ 1. Why did the rabbit cross the road?

____ 2. Why did the farmer cross the road?

____ 3. Why did the gum cross the road?

____ 4. Why did the robot cross the road?

____ 5. Why did the dinosaur cross the road?

____ 6. Why did the lemur cross the road?

____ 7. Why did the cow cross the road?

____ 8. Why did the elephant cross the road?

____ 9. Why did the frog cross the road?

____ 10. Why did the dolphin cross the road?

A. Chickens weren't invented yet.

B. To get to the udder side

C. It was stuck to the chicken's foot.

D. Somebody toad him to.

E. To get to the other tide

F. It was the chicken's day off.

G. To bring back his chicken

H. To prove she could hip hop

I. To take care of some monkey business

J. He was programmed to.

Art by Jannie Ho

Answers

1 The *Purr*-fect Trip
The cats went to
THE CANARY ISLANDS.

3 Where R U Going?
1. Atlanta, Georgia
2. Miami, Florida
3. Syracuse, New York
4. Milwaukee, Wisconsin
5. Indianapolis, Indiana
6. Fargo, North Dakota
7. Seattle, Washington
8. Philadelphia, Pennsylvania
9. Omaha, Nebraska

5 Critter Cruise
Eight passengers will be aboard after Birdboro.

6–7 Hidden Pictures®

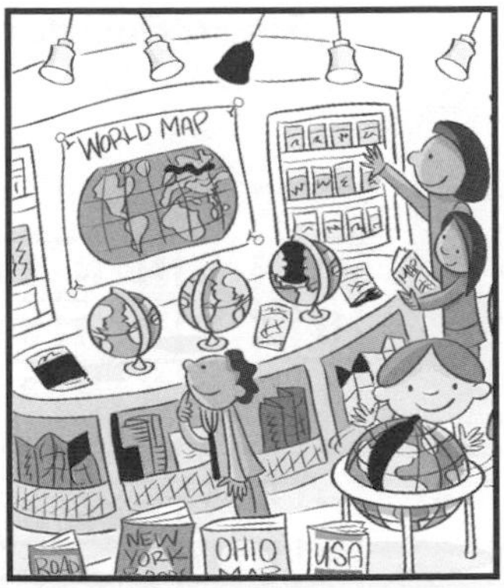

What do maps and fish have in common?
BOTH HAVE SCALES.

9 Reading Space

11 City Sounds
What runs through a city without moving? **ROADS**

12 Vacation Destinations
1. G, **2.** D, **3.** F, **4.** A, **5.** H, **6.** B, **7.** E, **8.** C

13 Family Vacations
Jennifer and William Green: NYC
Daniel and Emily King: Hawaii
Mia and Mike Peña: Alaska

15 All Aboard!
How are a train and an orchestra alike? **EACH HAS A CONDUCTOR.**

How do train engines learn to play sports? **THEY HAVE COACHES.**

Answers

15 Riddle Sudoku

Letters: A H E K N I

H	E	I	N	A	K
N	A	K	I	E	H
K	I	N	E	H	A
E	H	A	K	N	I
A	K	E	H	I	N
I	N	H	A	K	E

What does a choo-choo train need?
A HANKIE

17 Elephant Crossing

Why do elephants have trunks?
BECAUSE THEY LOVE TRAVELING

19 Trail Treading

What ice-cream flavor do bikers like the least? **ROCKY ROAD**

20 Just Sayin' . . .

21 The "You Night Did" States

1. Colorado
2. Wyoming
3. Illinois
4. Georgia
5. Hawaii
6. Maryland
7. Massachusetts
8. Mississippi
9. Oregon
10. Rhode Island

Bonus: Thank you, Ethan! I cracked the codes! Sincerely, Melanie

23 Boating Blunders

What did the boy get when he leaned over the back of the boat?
A STERN WARNING

25 Check...and Double Check

Answers

27 Road Trip on Planet Paint

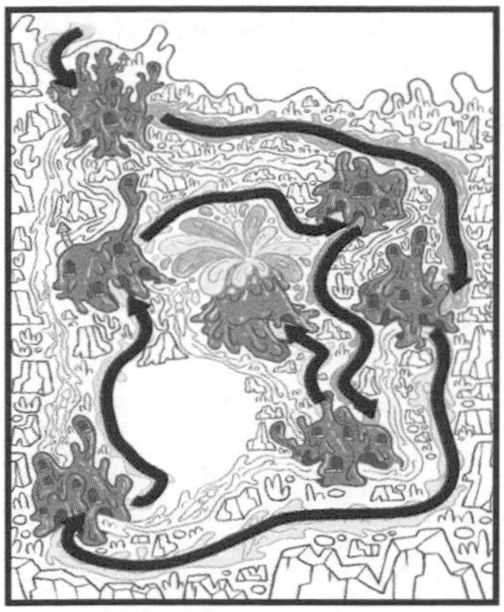

We made it to FINISH in seven moves. Perhaps you found another route.

BONUS: There are 6 pink brushes, 5 green brushes, and 4 orange brushes.

28–29 Hidden Pictures®

KNOCK, KNOCK.
WHO'S THERE?
DESPAIR.
DESPAIR WHO?
DESPAIR TIRE IS FLAT!

30 World Pieces

1. MEXICO
2. ARGENTINA
3. SWEDEN
4. ETHIOPIA
5. THAILAND

What travels around the world but never leaves its corner?
A STAMP

31 Robot Vacation

Why did the robot go on vacation?
TO RECHARGE HIS BATTERIES

33 Rush Hour

Answers

34 Just Sayin' . . .

35 Letter Road

What has cities without houses, rivers without water, and forests without trees?

A MAP

36–37 Hidden Pictures®

Why do birds fly south for the winter?

IT'S TOO FAR TO WALK.

38 Compass Code

Where's the best place to eat while hiking? **WHERE THERE'S A FORK IN THE ROAD**

39 Getting Around

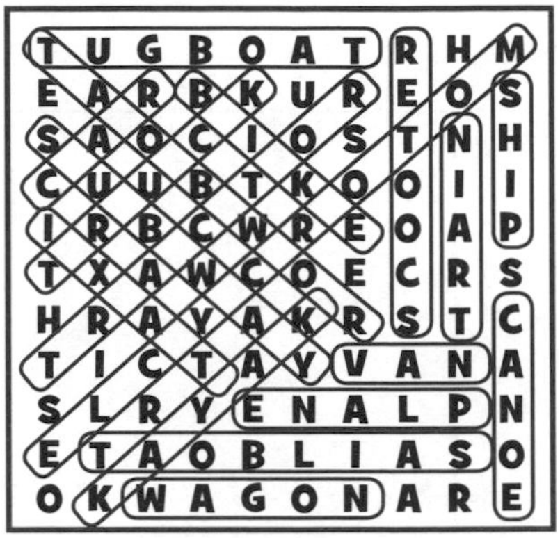

How does a lion paddle his canoe?

HE USES HIS ROAR.

41 A Message from the Past

Why did the pioneers cross the country in covered wagons?

BECAUSE THEY DID NOT WANT TO WAIT FORTY YEARS FOR A TRAIN

43 Ferry Ride

What do you call a story about boats? **A FERRY TALE**

44 Books Never Written

1. H, **2.** D, **3.** E, **4.** I, **5.** J, **6.** C, **7.** A, **8.** B, **9.** G, **10.** F

45 Truck Tunes

What do long-distance truckers listen to?

CROSS-COUNTRY MUSIC

Answers

46 Just Sayin' . . .

47 Riddle Sudoku

Letters: OTERCK

R	K	T	E	C	O
C	O	E	R	T	K
K	R	C	T	O	E
T	E	O	K	R	C
O	T	K	C	E	R
E	C	R	O	K	T

What only starts to work after it's fired?
A ROCKET

48 Car Carriers

What would happen if all the cars in the country were painted pink?
It would be a **PINK CAR-NATION.**

49 Freeway Free-for-All

What driver never drives a car?
A SCREWDRIVER

51 Hidden Words

KNOCK, KNOCK.
WHO'S THERE?
CANOE.
CANOE WHO?
CANOE COME OUT AND PLAY?

52 Racecar Riddles

1. What will the school for racecars do after the summer?
RE-ZOOM
2. What did the hot dog say when it finished the race first?
"I'M THE WIENER!"
3. Where do racecars go to wash their clothes?
THE LAUNDRY VROOOM

53 Truck Talk Box Drop

What did the tire say to the driver?
"GIVE ME A BRAKE."

Answers

54–55 **My Vacation on Earth**

EARTH
PIZZA
CIRCLE
PEPPERONI
MUSHROOMS
SWIMMING
WATER
ROCKS
HOME

Where does an alien park his vehicle? **AT A PARKING METEOR**

57 **Who's There?**

KNOCK, KNOCK.
WHO'S THERE?
ALPACA.
ALPACA WHO?
ALPACA THE TRUNK, YOU PACK-A THE SUITCASE.

59 **Look Both Ways!**

1. H, **2.** G, **3.** C, **4.** J, **5.** A,
6. I, **7.** B, **8.** F, **9.** D, **10.** E

"I call the seat by the window!"

"Somewhere cold."

Art by Bob Vojtko

More Travel-Size Fun for on the Go!

Need more puzzles to take with you? There are tons more in our Puzzlemania® Puzzle Pads series. You'll find mazes, wordplay, secret codes, brainteasers, and more!

COLLECT THEM ALL!

Word Searches
ISBN: 978-1-62979-423-5

Riddle Sudoku
ISBN: 978-1-62979-697-0

Maze Craze
ISBN: 978-1-62979-698-7

Brain Teasers
ISBN: 978-1-62979-422-8

Picture Puzzles
ISBN: 978-1-62979-424-2

Crazy Codes
ISBN: 978-1-62979-425-9

Cross Words
ISBN: 978-1-62979-834-9

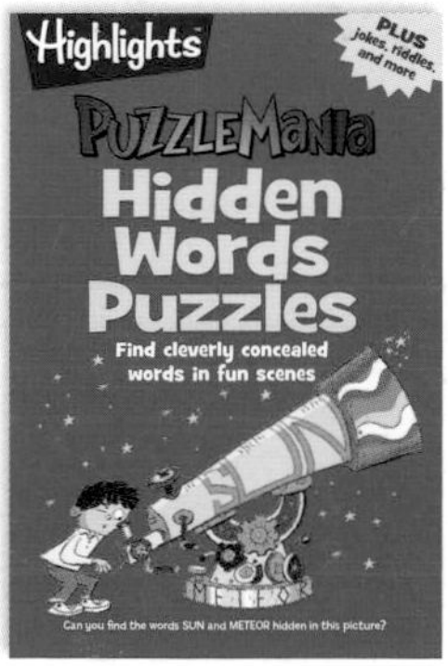

Hidden Words Puzzles
ISBN: 978-1-62979-833-2

Why do elephants have trunks?

Turn to page 17 to find out.

On-the-Go Jokes

Take this pad of jokes and puzzles everywhere you go to tickle your funny bone with laughs about things on the move.

Nobody does puzzles like Highlights™!

You'll also like:

ISBN: 978-1-62979-553-9

ISBN: 978-1-629

Keep laughing! Visit HighlightsKids.com

P.O. Box 18201 Columbus, Ohio 43218-0201
Printed in China
ISBN: 978-1-62979-835-6
First edition
10 9 8 7 6 5 4 3

$4.99 U.S. / $6.99
ISBN 978-1-62979-835-6
50499
9 781629 798356